Be MERRY

WRITTEN & COMPILED BY AMELIA RIEDLER • DESIGNED BY HEIDI RODRIGUEZ

COMPENDIUM®
INCORPORATED

live inspired.®

FIND THE MERRIMENT ALL AROUND YOU.

When we look for what makes us merry, we find what matters most to us: love, generosity, connection, gratitude, and each other. The holidays give us a special season of love, sharing, warmth, and connection—and the wonderful chance to remember that merriment is always within our reach, all the year through.

Here's to rediscovering the simple joys of spending time with each other, to participating fully in our lives. To embracing one another. To opening our hearts. To offering help to those who may need it. To saying thank you for blessings already given. To receiving joy. To finding ways to be merry. Every day of the year.

From home to home, and heart to heart, from one place to another.
The warmth and joy of Christmas, brings us closer to each other.

EMILY MATTHEWS

Welcome love and

HAPPINESS.

...KNOW THE JOY, FEEL THE WARMTH,
SHARE THE SWEETNESS,
AND CELEBRATE THE GIFT!

Douglas Pagels

Open your

HEART

to the season.

BE MERRY.

BE LOVING.

CHRISTMAS, A DAY WHEN CHEER AND GLADNESS BLEND, WHEN HEART MEETS HEART, AND FRIEND MEETS FRIEND.

J. H. Fairweather

DELIGHT IN THE TIME WHEN LOVED ONES ARE NEAR.

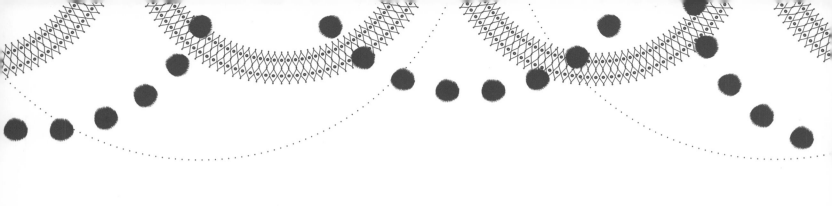

Having a place to go is a home.
Having someone to love is a family.
Having both is a blessing.

DONNA HEDGES

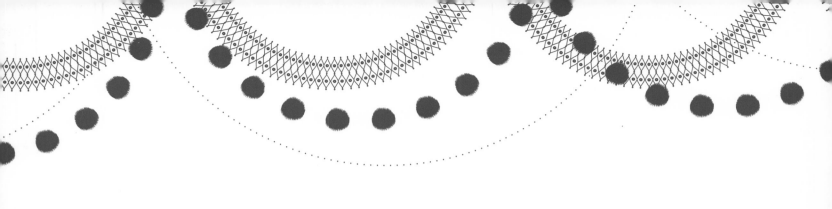

Take time to

ENJOY

each other.

BLESSED IS THE SEASON WHICH ENGAGES THE
WHOLE WORLD IN A CONSPIRACY OF LOVE!

Hamilton Wright Mabie

Notice

LOVE

everywhere.

MAY LIFE'S GREATEST GIFTS ALWAYS BE YOURS—
HAPPINESS, MEMORIES, AND DREAMS.

Josie Bissett

· ·

REFLECT ON THE JOYS OF THE PAST YEAR.

· ·

THE MORE YOU LOVE, THE MORE
LOVE YOU ARE GIVEN TO LOVE WITH.

Lucien Price

SHARE

your heart.

Happy, happy Christmas...

CHARLES DICKENS

SAVOR

every moment.

BE MERRY.

BE GENEROUS.

CHRISTMAS IS NOT AS MUCH ABOUT OPENING OUR
PRESENTS AS OPENING OUR HEARTS.

Janice Maeditere

OFFER KINDNESS.

THE MANNER OF GIVING IS
WORTH MORE THAN THE GIFT.

Pierre Corneille

GIVE

from the heart.

...LET IN THE SUNSHINE OF
GOODWILL AND KINDNESS.

Orison S. Marden

Share your

GENEROSITY

with those who need it most.

LET THERE BE PEACE ON EARTH, AND LET IT BEGIN WITH YOU.

Douglas Bloch

....

SPREAD PEACE.

....

Goodwill is reciprocal. The good thoughts you send out to others will return to you multiplied.

GRENVILLE KLEISER

Encourage

GOODNESS.

JOY IS THE TRUE GIFT OF CHRISTMAS...

Pope Benedict XVI

Seek

JOY.

BE MERRY.

BE CONNECTED.

IT IS CHRISTMAS IN THE HEART THAT PUTS CHRISTMAS IN THE AIR.

W.T. Ellis

··

KEEP A FESTIVE SPIRIT.

··

A GOOD FRIEND IS A CONNECTION TO LIFE...

Lois Wyse

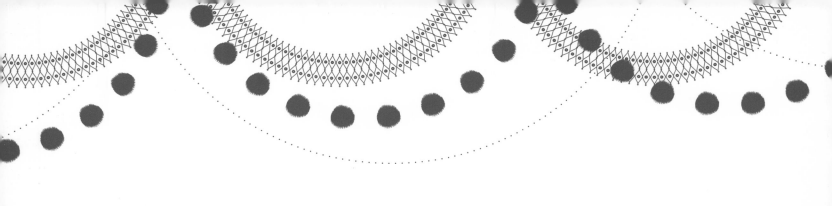

CHERISH

good friends, old and new.

WINTER IS THE TIME FOR COMFORT...FOR HOME.

Edith Sitwell

Feel the

WARMTH

that loved ones bring.

GIFT-BEARING, HEART-TOUCHING, JOY-BRINGING CHRISTMAS...

Unknown

....

FIND HAPPINESS
IN CONNECTION.

....

TIME ENDEARS BUT CANNOT FADE THE
MEMORIES THAT LOVE HAS MADE.

Unknown

REMEMBER

those you'll always love.

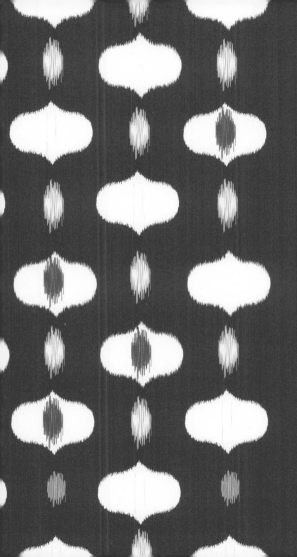

Christmas is a day of meaning and traditions, a special day spent in the warm circle of family and friends.

Margaret Thatcher

HONOR

heartfelt traditions.

BE MERRY.

BE THANKFUL.

AS LONG AS WE KNOW IN OUR HEARTS WHAT
CHRISTMAS OUGHT TO BE, CHRISTMAS IS.

Eric Sevareid

APPRECIATE ALL BLESSINGS.

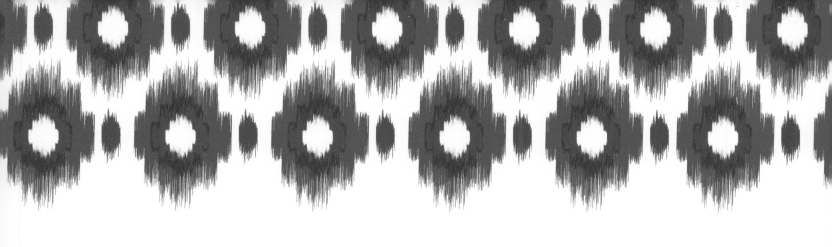

May your walls know joy; may every room hold laughter and every window open to great possibility.

MARY ANNE RADMACHER

EMBRACE
love and laughter.

ANY PLACE THAT WE LOVE BECOMES OUR WORLD.

Oscar Wilde

Be GLAD where you are.

HAPPINESS IS BEING AT PEACE, BEING WITH LOVED ONES...

Johnny Cash

· ·

CELEBRATE THOSE YOU LOVE.

· ·

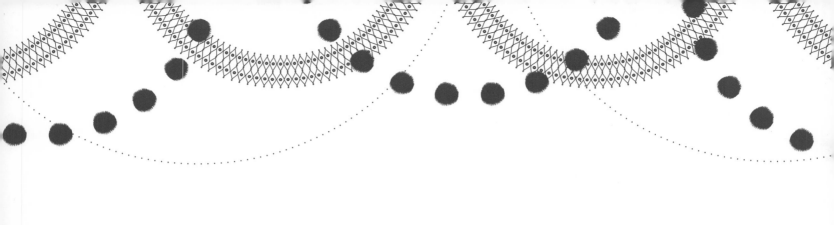

MAY HEAVEN SEND YOU MANY, MANY HAPPY DAYS.

William Shakespeare

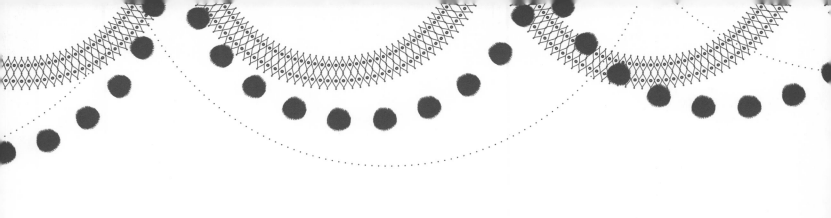

Anticipate

GOOD

things.

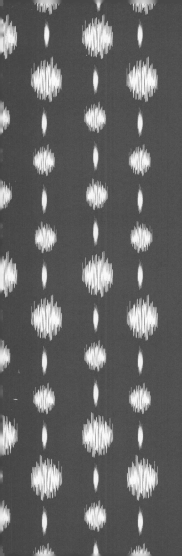

Here's wishing you more happiness
Than all my words can tell,
Not just alone for Christmas
But for all the year as well.

CHRISTMAS TOAST

Look forward to the future with

HOPE

and delight.

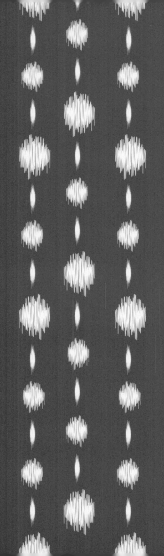

WITH SPECIAL THANKS TO THE ENTIRE COMPENDIUM FAMILY.

CREDITS:

WRITTEN & COMPILED BY: AMELIA RIEDLER

DESIGNED BY: HEIDI RODRIGUEZ

EDITED BY: M.H. CLARK

CREATIVE DIRECTION BY: JULIE FLAHIFF

ISBN: 978-1-935414-87-2

1st printing. Printed in China with soy and metallic inks.